"Legacy is in the lessons passed down."

These Pearls Are Real

by Carla M. Cherry

———— THE SECOND EDITION ————

iiPUBLISHING

These Pearls Are Real
Copyright © 2021 by Carla M. Cherry

Second Edition

Copyright notice
All rights reserved. No part of this book may be reproduced in any form or by any electronic or mechanical means, including information storage and retrieval systems, without permission in writing from the author or publisher, except for the use of brief quotations in a book review.

Cover design by tonii

ISBN: 978-1-7362167-6-7

Printed in the United States of America

iiPUBLISHING
New York, NY
www.toniiinc.com

Acknowledgements

This book, as always, is dedicated to the memory of those who have joined the Village of the Ancestors, especially my father, Melvin L. Cherry. I am forever grateful to my mother, my son Khari, my niece Anike, my sister Donna, my sister-friends Tanya Manning-Yarde and Soraya Angulo, and to Rainmaker. Thank you brother, for listening.

CONTENTS

A Mother's Gift	1
Morning Ritual	2
Girlhood Dreaming	3
Age Six	4
Sisterly Mischief	5
The Competitor	6
Cousins	7
Practice	8
Longing	9
Every May	10
Down South	11
Autumn Yield	12
For Little Black Girls	13
On the Block	15
False	16
Sister to Sister, Remixed	18
Mother and Son	19
The Talk	20
The Merit of Color	21
The Rush	22
Battle of the Seasonal Blues	23
Spring Lullaby	24
Hair Journey	25
Locs	26
In Remembrance	27
Trash	29
When the Student Teaches	30
Reborn	32
To Be Extraordinary	33

A Writing Life	34
Lift	35
Submission	36
Awakening	38
Solitude	39
Inkling	40
Closing the Rift	41
Courting	42
Twixt	43
She Was the One	44
This Queen	45
A Jar of Jerk	47
This New Day	48
Shine	50
Magic Man	53
Open Letter	54
Manifest	55
Raw	57
Opening	58
Vainglory	59
Case of Oranges	61
Day Shift/Night Shift	62
Nude	63
Au Naturel	64
O	65
Revealed	66
Something New	67
Before You Let Go	68

Let It Be	69
Virtuoso	70
Aftermath	71
Satisfaction	72
Naughty Girl	73
Bursts of Blue	74
Fantasy	76
The Real	77
Aquamarine	78
Authentic Woman	79
Whet	80
For My Valentine	81
When It's Love	82
Soothing Rain	83
In These Middle Years	84
Dreaming of Summer	85
Security	86
A Sunday Morning	87
A Summer Day in the Bronx	88
When She's in Remission	89
Trees of Everlasting Life	91
Flip	92
The Mother	94
Once	95
One and a Half Million and Counting	96
A Vegan's Dilemma	97
Happiness's Whisper	99

March 8	100
Hindsight	103
Good, or Nothing	104
Me, Too	106
For Bella	109
Things	110
Appropriation of Despair	112
Mea Culpa	113
Discovery	115
In Disguise	116
Time Out	119
April 4, 2017	121
Homegoing	122
Case Closed: April 4, 2018	123
Façade	124
Weight	126
Blue Funk	128
Woke	132
Continuum	135
A Daughter Speaks	136
She Wanted to Become a Nurse	142
Closing the Gap	144
Hold	146
A Hymn To The Evening	150
Seed	152
Afterword & The Author	*156*

These Pearls Are Real is about love and liberation. This medley of poems exalts the joys of childhood, self-acceptance, falling in love, grappling with gun violence, cultural appropriation, police brutality, and the neglect of the mentally ill. This poetry collection is like a bouquet of potpourri. May you find rejuvenation in the following pages.

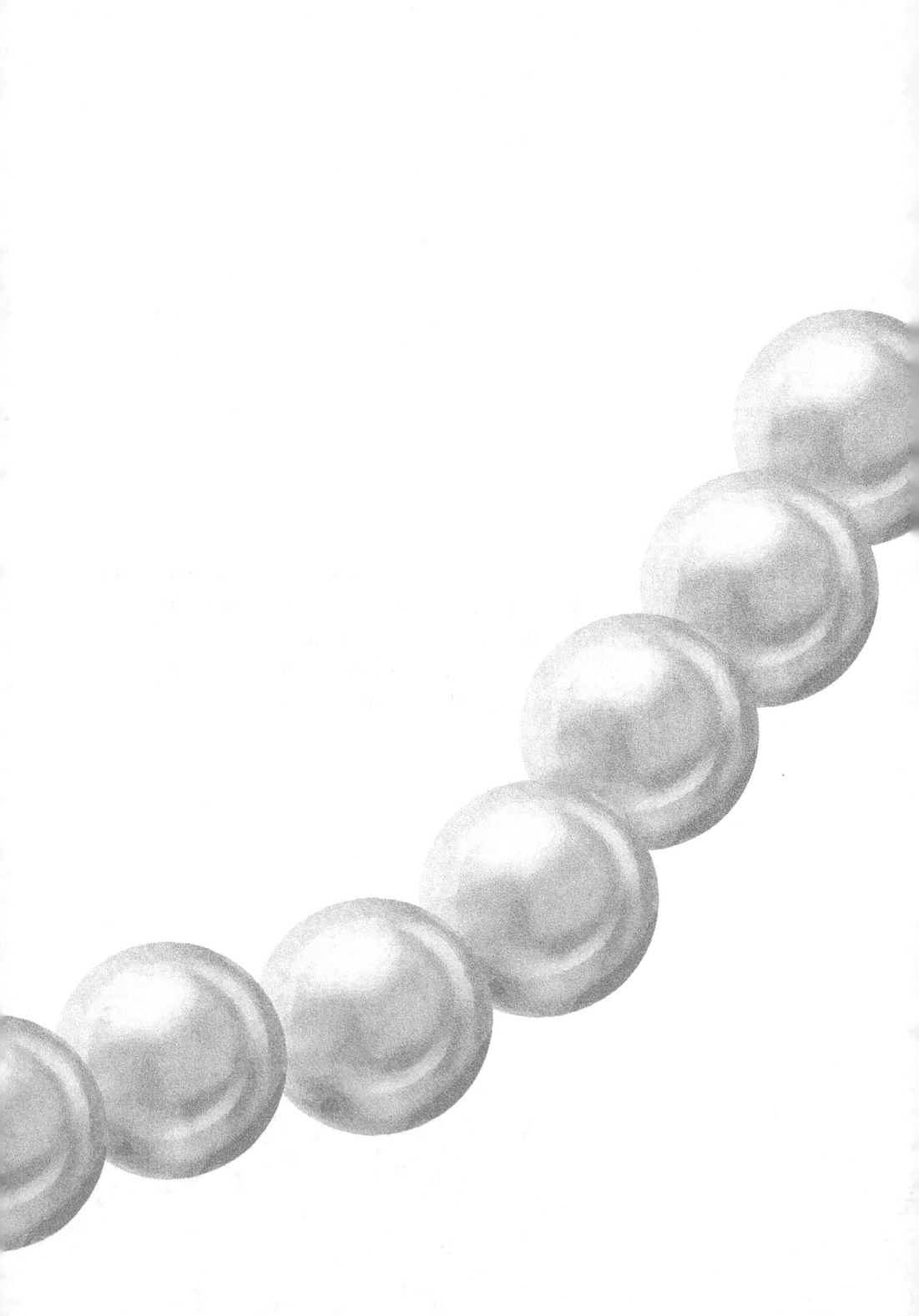

A Mother's Gift

Daughter.
Beautiful. Rare.
Like a **rainbow**.

The sweet, necessary pain
of your suckle.
I eat well, but
I pray there is enough
courage, purpose, power
for you
in my **milk**.

Earth is exquisite;
life is war.
Bacteria, the wicked, war hawks
will try to kill you.

Beloved,
you are no **minnow**.
Fight.
Win.

Morning Ritual

So she would know
she is
first light,
spark of hope
in darkness,
they named her **Dawn**.

Mornings,
her father
stood her in front
of the mirror before
they left for school:

Who is Daddy's most precious gift?

I am!
she'd exclaim.

And who shall you **camouflage**
your beauty, your wisdom for?

No one!

Girlhood Dreaming

Rubbernecking daily
at far-flung lights in blue-black sky,
if they were in her ambit,
if she had the proper **vessel**--
stairs,
a **ladder,**
a rocket;

if she wouldn't
burn or freeze her fingertips
she would hold
the blue supergiant/
red dwarf/
white dwarf stars
in her hands
and watch them glow.

Age Six

"Hold my hand,".
Mother's **chant**,
at Daughter's loosening grip,
to dash after this/that, until
the footlong twig.

Damp sand.
Daughter wrote:
Love.
Peace.
Hope.

Daughter's eyes
gleamed golden oak in the sun.
Mother lifted her,
waded hip-deep,
mingling laughter as waves bombarded them.

Hummed in Daughter's ear
as Ocean washed away
Mother's/Daughter's **cursive** dreams.

Sisterly Mischief

Car windows were **mirrors**,
reflecting our brown beauty.

When they were foggy
from rain/body heat,
we drew our names,
hearts,
animals,
a small **garden** of flowers
in the mist
before Daddy compelled their erasure.

His eyes back on the road,
our mouths formed the letter O.
Blew.
Drew again in our **vapor**, victorious.

The Competitor

He **open**ed the deck of **cards**.
Held them in his six-year-old hands
like a **clamp**
as he studied his grandmother's face.
Shuffled.
Dealt.
With each hand,
she had nothing he needed.
"Go fish," she sang.
He frowned and was near tears.
"I'm not giving up, Grandma.
I will never win if I quit."

Cousins

The fan only **circulated**
hot air around the living room,

but the grown-ups still arranged
the dining room chairs in rows
before our impromptu stage--
a blanket thrown over
the dining room table
for **cover**.

We children sat underneath
and giggled as we each waited
for our **debut**
to sing crooked notes
and dance offbeat.

Practice

Gentle twisting/pushing
foot joint, head joint.
Spine, pencil straight.

She **swallowed**.
Pursed lips against lip plate.

Delicate puffs of dry air divided--
floating down/through the body,
curved fingers pressing keys/**valves**,
the rhythm of her clicking nails,
fused with breathy imitation of the
full/half/quarter notes on the page.

An ensemble of one.

Longing

One **spring** night,
not long after Daddy died--
alone in bed,
in rapid-eye-movement sleep,
I felt a presence
hug me tightly.

Some might say
it was my grief
camouflaged by a dream
but ever since
I have sought a supernatural force
to **tap**,
to induce that presence,
that fatherly embrace

Every May

Crescent moons underwhelm.
I gaze/gape
at full moons,
curved like my belly before
I bled/cried/thrust my son
into this giant blue ball
of joy and pain.

Had I a magic **wand**,
each Flower Moon,
I would conjure a Kind **Reaper**,
who would convene the spirits
of my many long-gone mothers.
Just to talk.

Down South

I loved our family
drives to North Carolina,
digging through photo albums
in the **basements** of elderly
aunts and uncles,

being called thrice daily
for soul food
and sweet tea.

Sweaty play in summer heat.
Resting under oaks,
birds' **nests** on high.

Snatching fireflies
from their romantic overtures,
their lights in our hands.

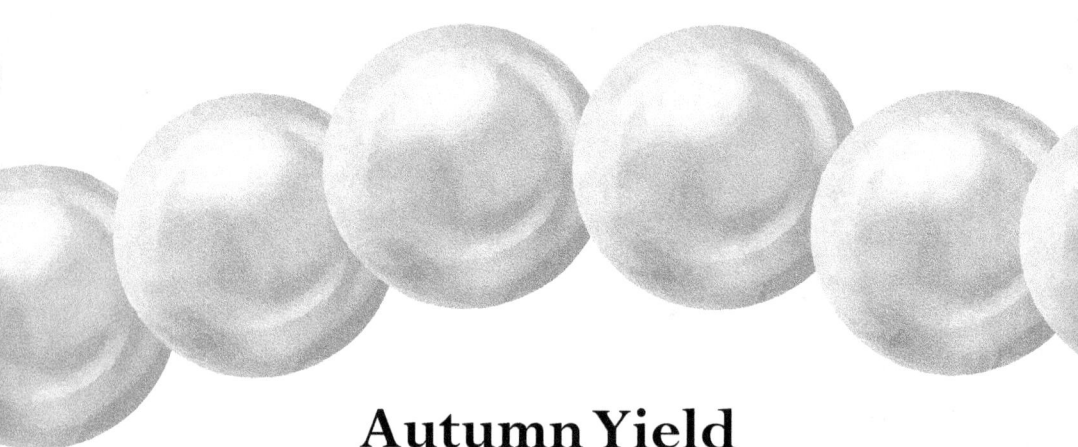

Autumn Yield

I imagine
Grandfather and Grandmother
during harvest:
descending the **stairs**
at daybreak,
him strolling his **wheatfield**,
nestling the stalks between
his calloused fingers,
Grandmother
pinching corn kernels,
rasping the silk.
Scythes swinging.
My father/uncles
bundling, then
loading the bushels
on the truck,
driving to town,
delivering their love and sweat
for sale.

For Little Black Girls

If she had a daughter, none of
those **rainbow**-colored
barrettes for her hair;

those **cords**
were wrapped into metal
bands that pulled her hair into
the folds.

If she had a daughter,
she would have
cornrowed, flat-twisted,
plaited her tresses,

sometimes letting them fly as
she played outside until
streetlights flickered for the
dusky shouting of **names**.

On the Block

We girls, outside,
playing music,
talking, teasing.

He came.
Goaded my friend,
laughing about how her mother
almost got raped in her building's **basement**.

She balled up her fists,
danced in his **shadow**,
screamed, "Come on!"
as we held on to our **heroine**,
guarding her five feet, few inches
from his muscular six feet.

False

We girls, my sister and I, were sheltered, safely touched--hugs, kisses on cheeks.
Saturday mornings, feet neatly tucked underneath thighs in front of the TV, singing the theme song, laughing at Fat Albert, Mushmouth, Dumb Donald and Weird Harold--"If you're not careful, you might learn something before it's done."
Cosby Show, every Thursday night at 8. Parents, side-by-side with us on the sofa.
Daddy loved Cliff's expensive patterned sweaters.

It was strangers that our parents worried about,

creeps that might lure us with candy/snatch us off the street.
Bragged Congressman Conyers brought us the King Holiday, Congressional Black Caucus. Rapped along with Run DMC, the Fat Boys, L.L. Cool J. when I saw Krush Groove. Loved Harvey Weinstein's films: Fruitvale Station, The Great Debaters, Mandela: Long Walk to Freedom, the Spike documentary about Kalief Browder. Charlie Rose interviewed the greats: Raoul Peck to Charles Blow to Neil DeGrasse Tyson.
Lupita Nyong'o, Terry Crews, Jenny Lumet, Angelina Jolie, Gwyneth Paltrow, showed us:
Beware those who entertain, inform, reassure, via television, radio, film; those who employ, who rule.

It was the strangers our parents worried about,

not the limo that took her to his home instead of hers. Commands: Drink this. Swallow that. Rape. Forced fellatio. The penis/breast/butt groping. Unwelcome hands on legs, through pants. Business done in his home. Uninvited nudity, invitations to join his shower. Don't tell, or else.
We must teach our daughters, our sons: enthusiastic consent, bodily autonomy, and:
Be unafraid to speak up, even though Roy Moore and his ilk are still in, Franken is out. Let us demand prosecutors indict the rich/powerful as vigorously as the poor. All this time,

it was the strangers that our parents worried about.

Sister to Sister, Remixed

Afraid he would
feel at home
between other thighs,
she stuck to him
like **wallpaper**.

He announced the end,
unmoved by each **drip**
of her tears.

I told her:
I used to put **gel** in my hair
so the style would stay.

I stopped because
it got sticky,
made my tresses hard.
Understand?

Mother and Son

Since your shoulders
surpassed my head,
dreams diverged from mine,
been **crystal-ball** clear
you're a man.

America's appetite
for black flesh, the
ad infinitum list of names,
compelled my vise grip
on this invisible umbilical **cord**,
desire to wrap you in a **cocoon**.

It's confinement
nevertheless.

You're ready.
Go.
Be.

The Talk

Son. Daughter.
Be discerning through
these ticklish urges/yearnings.

The womb be sacred space
for fecund **eggs** to cling to,
be fed with blood/love's dawning.

The birth canal be
holy **vessel** as our babies
are thrust into this
cauldron of opposition:
good and evil,
joy and sorrow,
pleasure and suffering,
and everything in between.

The Merit of Color

Momma used to say
white walls
make everything look clean.

Bored, I bought
a painting
of a **rainbow**.

Held it
flush against the wall,
before I hung it,

imagined sunlight
beaming through the window
reflecting its colors,
pretty prisms on my floors
during the days,
kaleidoscopic **shadows**
at night.

The Rush

Arose at **dawn**,
rays of sun
splintered
against skyscrapers.

Did my brisk,
beat-the-clock walk,
waited for
green-yellow-red lights,
as cars **snaked** their way
around each other
and us.

One of these days
I want to arise at dawn,
watch rays of sun **splinter**
through trees,
water **snake** around thickets,
and my feet.

Battle of the Seasonal Blues

If Winter had
armpits
I would tickle them
so It would loosen
its grip.

Spring Lullaby

Last night
I cracked open
one window.
Wind was blowing
blades of my blinds
in gentle sway.
Watched them dance.
Fell asleep
to the echoes of tapping.

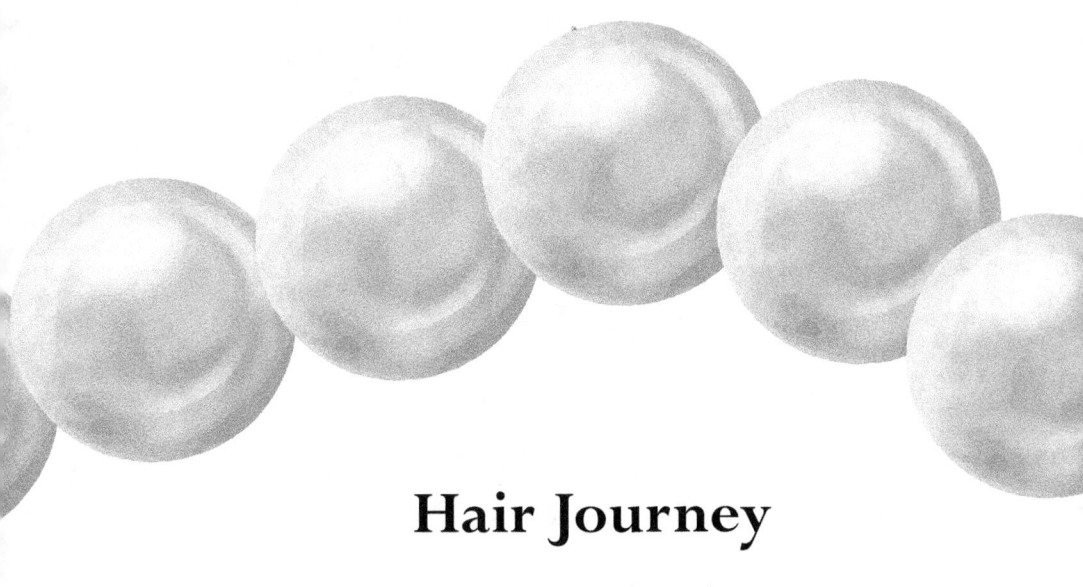

Hair Journey

I seldom let my hairstylist
blow dry, flat iron,
my hair.

It's cute
but a **drain**
when it gets sweaty, wet in the rain,
in the shower,
or swells underneath blazing sun.

Going to let it loc.
No more **camouflage** of its kink.
Will grow them long,
to **stream** across my shoulders,
caress my back.

Locs

Bought crochet hoods
to **deal** with
these straying strands of mine
until they decide to
intertwine into spirals
past my shoulder blades
but I, my man,
get a **kick** out of playing
in these kinks.

The crochet hoods
sit in my drawer.

Why conceal beauty
with a **veil**?

In Remembrance

She swallowed,
the brine of his lips
in her **spit**.

Cried herself into
slow wave sleep.
Awakened to every
artery ferrying blood/oxygen,
sunlight blazing
the **wallpaper**'s golden leaves.

Mirror manifested
locs cascading like Tokaleya Tonga
above bounteous bosom/hips.
She laughed at her amnesia.
Stretched her limbs.
Lit a bundle of sage.

Trash

I was cleaning out my dresser.

Found a picture of us in the bottom **drawer**.

I started to save it for my photo album
until I remembered how your **tongue**
got **tangled** whenever I asked you
say
I love you.

What a waste
of my smiling pose
paper
ink.

When the Student Teaches

It's Open School Night,
my classroom's been empty a while,
when my favorite student arrives with her mother.
Identical smiles,
onyx sparkles in their eyes,
cream-colored sweaters and black furry boots.
I laugh, exclaim,
"This is too cute! May I?"
They pose, I click a picture,
promised it will not go on the internet.
We three:
Me, American,
they Jamaican,
all of us of Afrikan descent,
applaud as I announce her A's in both classes she has with me.
I ask if her mother knows of our upcoming trip to see I Am Not Your Negro.
She says they watched it together, that
she always has her children watch documentaries about black history.
Got that trait from an Afrocentric aunt.
Good job Mom, I say.

The gleam from Jada's smile is a lodestar.
I am proud,
then suddenly, slightly sad
more of our girls don't,
that I didn't,
have Jada's style, her grace.

Fun loving girl.
Lip gloss and go,
but
loves to dress up: skirts and heels;
dress down: jeans and frilly tops.
Brushes her velutinous hair into an Afro puff,
or a weave with long tresses.

Even the most popular boy who calls women thots, bitches
surrenders those epithets when she passes by in the hallway--

She's shorty.
Don't call her that, I scold. She's a young lady.
He declares: Yo, that's wifey right there!
Miss, you gotta teach me to be a gentleman.
I laugh a little.
I teach English; will do what I can within 56 minutes.
Want to tell him he won't stand a chance.
It's not my place.
She's got it under control--laughter, firm no-thank-yous.

Faith and trust in self,
for the girls who are adored,
seem as natural as glossy skin
when you live beneath gleaming tropical sun.

At Jada's age,
couldn't fathom how to
delight in the arc of amber in my eyes,
my hair's natural array against my shoulders,
the shine of my smile,
slim figure, its ease in my clothes.

All my book smarts and skills,
spent so much adolescent time on the phone with my girlfriends,
lamenting the popular boys put off by my glasses, my acne--
Nah, nah, not her.
Years seeking love from men who I was good enough for
in the meantime.

In this past lustrum,
fell on and fractured my shoulder. I was told:
You have a lot of scar tissue.

Months spent with fingers deep-kneading muscles,
pondering probing questions.

How many times have you had a broken heart?

Should have walked past them all,
my chin perpendicular to my throat,
like Jada.

Reborn

There are things
we can know
for sure,
like
an **island**
is a piece of land
surrounded
by water.

As I sit here
in this pew

I pray this
tiny **vessel** of
grape juice
will wash
me clean, and
like **scissors**,
cut sin
from my blood
body
soul

To Be Extraordinary

I be,
my hope be,
my faith be,
my love be,
deep
like a spring,
like a river.

No tourists allowed.

A Writing Life

Looked for my scissors
everywhere.

Lately I all do is
write, read.
Books, papers, strewn about.

Heard the sound of cars
driving down slick streets.

Rain.

A good day to
clean, organize.

Sprayed my mirror with Windex.
Began wiping it down.

Saw my mother
in my face.

A poem
was born.

Lift

Before plugging my laptop into the socket to work on my poem,
I found a tiny crimson and black spotted hump
on the windowsill.

Whispered, "ooh, a ladybug".
As if my alto could shatter her antennae.

Got busy
googling symbolism.
Plotting on the luck that's on the way.
Foot-rubbing love, here to stay?
Pontificating on what other good fortune lives
beneath God's feathers and wings.

Forgot to open the window
so she could get back to climbing her rose bushes,
the delight of aphids.

When I checked the windowsill
I found
cloak,
faded to the color of brick.
Seven black spots
of sorrow.

Submission

Already been tapped
like a maple tree
by kind words and kisses
until my bark gave way,
revealing sap.
Promised comfort, security,
proudly watched my man
sip, swig, slurp, strengthen.
Satisfied, he sought other sweets.
So, the thought of ever
kneeling for anyone
other than God,
nodding to a man's yeses,
no's over my life,
my money,
makes my stomach flip over
like a car careening off a cliff.
These days I prefer

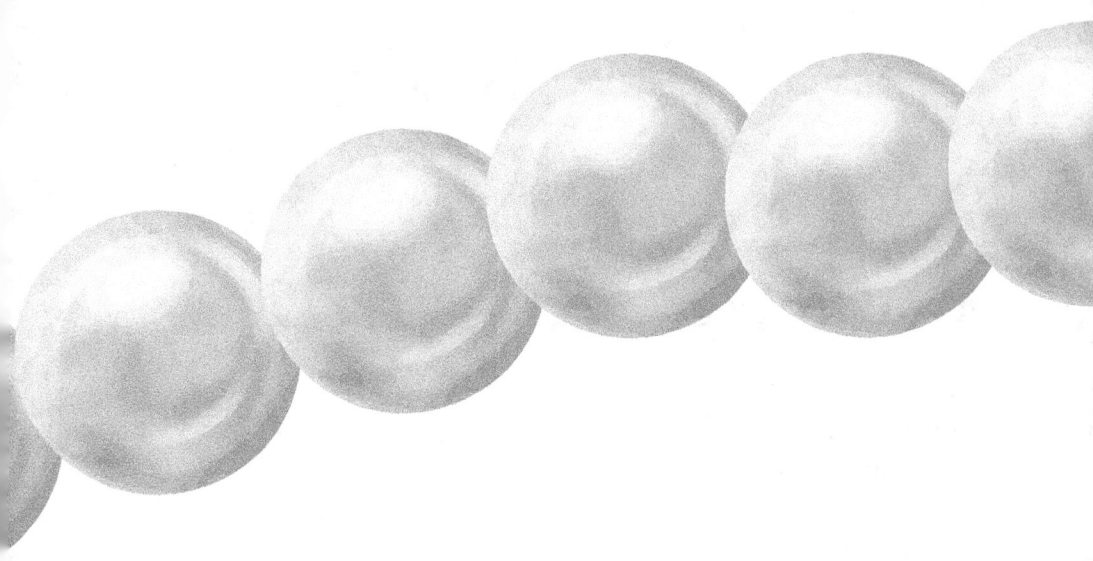

the kind of submission
where I am
catapulting these poetic snippets of my soul
into sibylline wilderness.
Each serotonin hit
from seeing my name
in black ink,
various fonts,
online and off,
satiates like sugar cane.
The rejections-- from strangers--
ain't got quite the same sting.
Still, waiting on replies
is like laying
in a barren, snowy field
watching for sunflowers
to blossom, to bloom.

Awakening

First buds of leaves
adorn tree branches
like miniature ornaments.

The flux of water
from icy thaw
snakes through
brooks/
streams/
ponds/
rivers.

Dandelions
Buttercups
Violets
peek shyly through grass
seeking the surging heat
of sunrays.

I sit,
hum
to the sparrow's trill,
finger the furbelow
of my skirt.

Solitude

Soft summer rains.
If alone,
I sit in my basement,
listen to droplets' rhythm.

Don my shortest, sleeveless
sundress, sandals that have
seen better days.

Walk through my grass,
God's tears trickling down
naked parts of my skin.

Amble through the house.

Marvel at the prints of my feet.

Mop up my hypocrisy.

Inkling

First date.

Strolled the riverside
beholding departing ships,
water licking their undersides.

Something pink, black
slithered along the road.
I recoiled.

"Rainbow snake.
Ain't poisonous."

He hoisted it.
"They don't bite."

It undulated
around his arm.

"Put her down",
I said.

"Just because
something's pretty
doesn't mean
you can touch it,".

Closing the Rift

If I could
build a temple
for our broken-hearted,
I would
paint cherubs
on its ceiling
with burnished bronze skin,
hair of wool,
wide noses,
full lips.

Their quivers would be
full of arrows
with tips
wrapped in rosemary.

They would aim deftly,
then, slice the air,
hit every target,
trigger sempiternal love.

Courting

I,
gun-shy,
he persistent:
posting
"Good mornings"
"Good evenings"
on my wall,
that poem
to my inbox
about easing
a red rose
in my hair.

I gave in.

We picked
a quiet spot
along the Hudson River.

He unfolded
the blanket,
offered me his hand,
helped me sit.
Grapes.
Wine.
That lingering kiss.

Twixt

He loves to play.
Our first time
I tangled myself
in the sheets
like a bottle of wine
at Christmas,
all wrapped in cellophane
tied up with a red velvet bow.

We giggled through
the unraveling
and ravaging.

No more cherub-cheeked men
for me.
Now I like them lean,
flat-bellied,
arms like twine.

She Was the One

First, she excused herself,
rubbed water and lavender soap
on her mouth
until her lipstick
was a memory.

When her blush-colored mouth
mingled with his,
all the other oral pleasures
he'd ever known were forgotten.

Five minutes passed
until the roar in his ears
had ceased.

This Queen

One lunar cycle of
hat-tipping,
polite greetings at dusk,
before he learned her name.

Year of
floral offerings,
long walks,
asking/answering
hundreds of questions,
before he tattooed every inch
of her skin with his lips.

She loves him for knowing
her body will never
be his kingdom.

Even now,
he asks,
"May I?"

A Jar of Jerk

Just out of the shower   he saw me putting away the
groceries.
Didn't even stop   to grab his towel.
Walked over to   my bent over back.
"Babe."

Led me away.   "Let me."
I watched him as he brought the bags into the kitchen
unpacked each item,   muscles flexing and contracting,
stroking bones;
a swinging organ   I love to play.
There is nothing quite like baby oil on brown skin.

He picked up   the jar of jerk paste.
"You only got mild?"   I said, "I wasn't sure if I could
handle the spicy kind.
I'm lucky if I can handle you."

He laughed.   "One Jamaican thing at a time," I
smiled.

"Flattery will get you everywhere."   I kissed the dimples at the small of
his back,

                             Wished it were a Saturday morning
so he could stay.

This New Day

I'm fat, I sigh, on those blue days,
while he is watching me swab my skin with lotion.
He shakes his head. "Man, your silhouette is crazy".
He reaches for my arm,
pulls me to the edge of the bed,
kisses the juicy swell below my hips.

And as he stirred from slumber this new morning,
he said he hears the sawing of redwoods
each time we sleep.
Sorry.
"For what?"
Turned over to face me.
Pinched his thumb and forefinger together.
Made a running caress along the billowy path
from my neck to navel.
"That is sexy as hell," he whispered.
Fixed hickory eyes on mine.
"You see--
a woman with a light, graceful snore,
bends easily on the things she believes.
But a woman who snores steadily,
like, a growl,
has a backbone."

Bathed in the orange glow of sunrise,
I raised up on an elbow.
Climbed on him.
Stroked the sickle buried
in his right eyebrow--the mark of Ogun.
Embroiled my fingers in
the black wooly tangle at the nape of his neck.
Kissed him feather-lightly.

Every woman should love,
be loved by at least one poet,
who morphs foibles/flaws into metaphor.

Shine

This is for you,
he said.
I nestled it inside my palm.

Brown agate,
color of a coffee bean,
size of my forefinger,
shaped like a teardrop, or
an icicle.

For protection.
You can put in your purse
or your pocket.

I have done neither,
afraid it will fall out
amid my constant fumbling--
keys, money, lipstick--
that I won't hear its light thud
on floors,
these New York City sidewalks, and streets.

It waits in my jewelry drawer,
until he makes a necklace
that will fall in the crevice of my breasts, shine,
radiate its energy to the chakra of my heart.
I will wear it daily.
It will
heal wounds,
keep me safe
when my love
is not around
to flex his sinewy muscles,
and swing,
if need be.

Magic Man

My heart was no empty vessel
when we met. But it's like he
waved a magic wand,
filled it past its brim
with a love radiating light like a pulsar,
mining my fears, hopes, dreams.
Listened.
Whispering aphorisms
about black beauty
and
oh, that occasional
caveman grip of my hair.

Mashing the mundane,
the momentous, into mountains for me to climb,
to find my spare tire,
learn to change it, my oil,
for those times he can't be there;
to lean into,
delight in the curve of winding roads;
Babe. They're a driver's dream. Trust your car, yourself;
to become my own boss:
You can start your own school.
Open a business. What kind would you want to do?
to triumph in the art of inditement/elaboration,
wield my pen with the same mastery
as my tongue nuzzling
his Adam's apple.
For many, it marks man's disobedience to God,
but I nuzzle his most nights,
to feel it brush against my cheek
when he swallows,
to hear his leonine growl
when I clamp my lips
on the right side of his neck, then the left,
in salty satisfaction.

Open Letter

Metals.
Solid, save
shimmering, silver
mercury.

You too, confound--
cajoling,
rebuffing me,
like the tow and ebb
of the ocean.

Love builds.
Love bruises.

We will never know
what ours can do
unless you stop running.

Even a panther is only
built for short sprints.
For prey.

Trust that I will stay.

Manifest

There was no ice to thaw.
Our love: a slow waltz
of ken,
warm hearts.
Couplings are celebrations:

One night,
His hands held my breasts
like two perfect crystal-balls.
He let them fall, said:
I like the seat of your breasts.

Gave suck
on the nibs of my nipples
as if I could feed him.

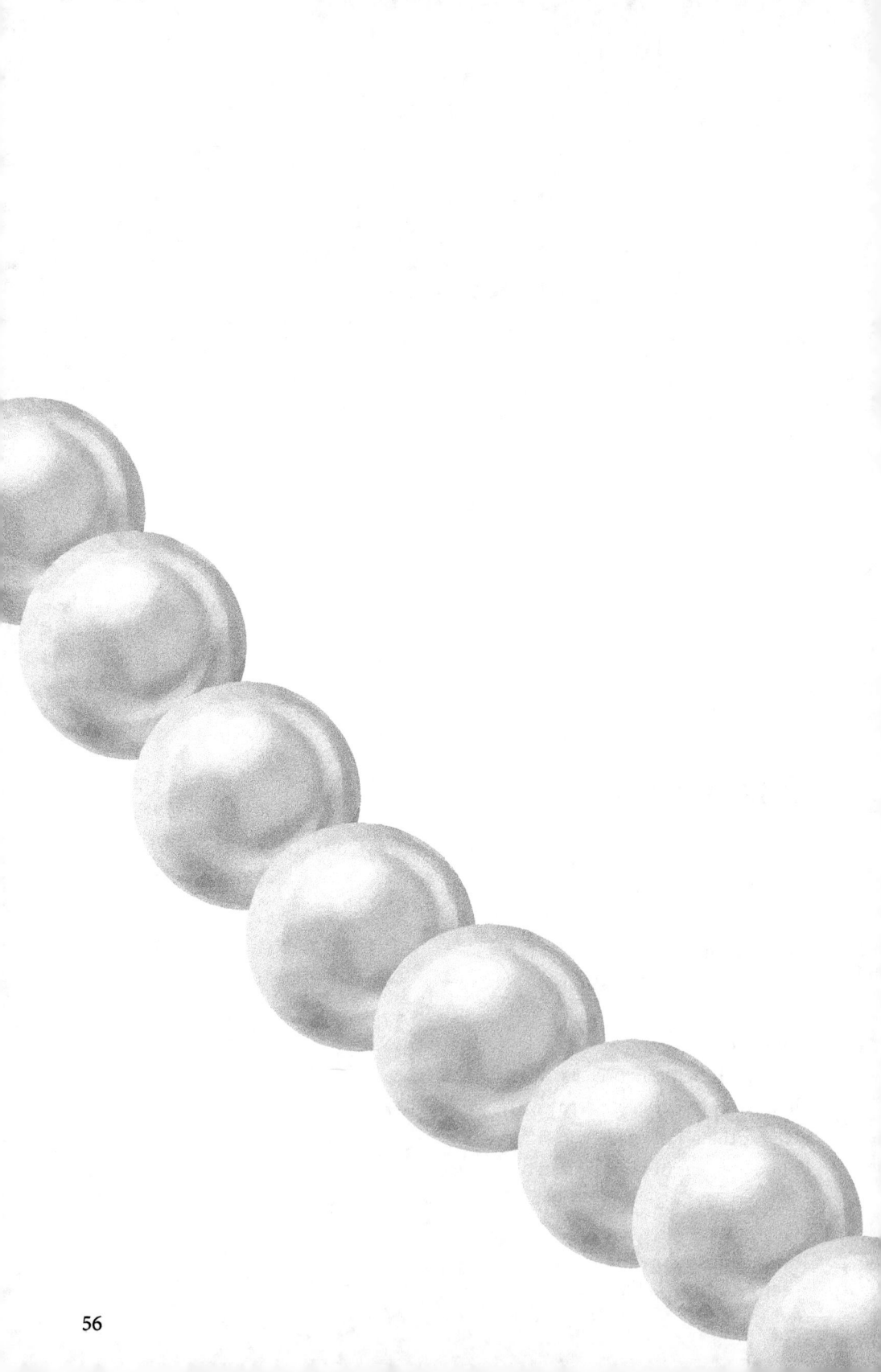

Raw

Funny.
The skin of our backs
is thicker than our fingertips;
so sensitive.
So itchy,
so hard to reach.
Awkward to find ways
to stretch my arms
back far enough for my fingernails
to hit the spots
and look dignified in public.

This morning he was awake,
and on the phone, so I whispered,
"Would you mind moisturizing my back?"
"Sure", he said, extending his hands
as I pumped out the peach-colored Palmer's Cocoa Butter.

As he spread it across my damp back,
I could feel it sinking into every crevice.
He smiled as I pushed my shoulders and neck back in relief.

That lotion smells like chocolate.
That's why he told his friend,
"Hold on, I gotta tell her goodbye,"
and he kissed my belly before
I squashed myself into my size 16 jeans.

Maybe those prickling tickles
in our shoulders, our spines
are God's way,
reminding us
we need each other to get at
those hard-to-reach places,
and how delicious it is to be loved.

Opening

Like scissors,
you pierced my essence

made my mask
fall away,
with
steady eye gazes while
I discuss my day,
hardy embraces while I sleep or cry,
promises we'll get through this,
the meals you cook,
and calling my name
so, I look up,
see your eyes sparkle
when you say, "I love you".

Vainglory

Used to think romance
was like
cursive handwriting--
beautiful,
but becoming obsolete.

Forgive me
for vaporing on--
but he poured love
into his hands,
flung it against my darkness;
there was light.

His words plant seeds.
He tickles me wet.

My life,
like an Edenic garden now,
in full bloom.

Case of Oranges

Our love
is like a case of oranges.

Every month a fresh one comes.
Every day, we eat,
peel the outer layers,
rive the wholes into sections,
savor citrus notes.
Each pulpy wedge
rewards:
nectarous nourishment
making us immune
to the swill of -isms
that surround,
that promise to swallow us whole.

When I wash the juice
from my hands
I try not to imagine
how hard it would be
if rot arrives,
deliveries cease,

how long it would take before
I find a love
this/more
fruitful
edifying
sweet

Day Shift / Night Shift

To mask light bite marks on her neck,
she pulled up the collar of her dress.

Head in her bosom.
Inhaled his hair.
He kissed her bottom lip.

Pressed between foreign flesh,
lemon vapor still in her nose,
she almost got off the train
to return to the comfort
of his Jamaican lilt and legs.

Nude

She was at the mirror.
Plum lipstick in hand.

He smiled.
"Nice, but baby,
you look and
taste beautiful
without it."

She lingered a moment.
Had forgotten
how much she loved
the natural chocolate shade
of her heart-shaped lips.

She kissed him.
Their sweaters touched.

A spark.

"Static electricity," he laughed.

"No babe. Just me."

Au Naturel

She gazed at the mirror,
blotted at the smears
of artery-red lipstick
on her chin,
at the residuum
of their tangled limbs--
steady rise and fall
of his chest as he slept.

She said aloud,
What do I need with makeup?

Got enough of love's glow
for my mouth
cheeks
eyes.

O

Spread the word,
she said.

Tell your brothers
not to double down
on the caress of their fingertips,
the angle
and force
of their thrust
after a slow glide
into The Garden.

The best door
to the high spot
is the octave rise
in the middle of
"I love you".

Revealed

It was the night
of her debut.

She forgot
her shyness.

She pulled down
the last of his clothes
sat him in their
oversized chair
like an emperor on his throne.

Tied the blindfold tautly.

She straddled him.

With her
fingertips
lips
swirling hips
she subdued
his speech,
his kingdom.

Something New

Her idea--
silk scarf wrapped around her wrists.
through the headboard's lattice.

Exploratory kisses,
nips with teeth
triggered her trembling.

The inability to rush his fingers
through circular motions,
was like turning on a tap.

He murmured marvel at her
slow drip
her taut embrace
their vigorous work towards
simultaneous eruption,
simultaneous roar.

Before You Go

Her arch,
undeniable.
Shaped like an apple,
and as sweet.

He had forgotten
to shift his shirt
out of the way.

Was wet with her juices.
Biggest spot
shaped like her backside,
wide like a rainbow.

He put on a fresh one.
She combed his hair.

Arch of his smile,
undeniable.

Let It Be

Thunderstorms aroused him.
He spooned her.

"I'll be back," she said.
Arose, headed for the bathtub.

"Please don't,".
No masking her natural aroma this time.

Cradled her hips in his hands.
His lips/tongue did their work.
Kissed her so she could taste her tang.

Entered her, like sunlight through raindrops.

A rainbow bespangled the sky.

Virtuoso

The brush was
his besom in this war with her shyness,
and with steady dips into the gold glitter,
he whisked
her forehead,
cheeks,
bosom,
navel,
and thighs.

Her hair was
a billowing black cloud
that she did not need to fix.

She cambered,
as he captured half-moons,
rondures,
and whorls
with his camera.

Aftermath

As she slept,
he stood in the shower
water droplets stroking
everywhere she had been,
admiring the arc of lipstick,
reconjuring the rush of blood
to his head,
beyond,
below,

mystified/gratified
that no matter his angle,
speed of his thrust,
as he rollicked against
her ridges and valleys,
he couldn't fully
pry her loose.

Satisfaction

Light from the New Moon,
morning glory from their garden in hand,
purple petals licked every limb
until he stirred:
"Babe, I'm thirsty."

"Water. Too much juice isn't good. Too much sucrose."

He bounded out of bed.
Scooped her up,
laid her down,
hands on her knees.

"You're never too much sugar.
Protein, either."

Naughty Girl

Nothing like having
a pitcher of lemonade
to myself.

In my juvenescent moods,
I overwhelm
my favorite tumbler,
swallow after desperate swallow
of citrus elixir,
pausing to gasp for air

little rivers of tangy-sugary juice
cascading down my chin,
snickering about who
will come home next
and cry out,
"Who drank it all?"

Bursts of Blue

Got three-fourths of a container of blueberries I bought
to sweeten the oatmeal I would otherwise be gagging,
and for the anthocyanin.
Good for the joints.
Sometimes my knees lightly pop and creak.

My silky skin is secretive, but I will confess it--
I'm at that age when we worry about fiber/iron/protein and inflammation.

I like pinching these deep purple orbs to check their firmness,
their light bounce in my hand while I run them through cool water.

I am going to make a blueberry pie.
I had it for the first time this year.
It was a chilly January day that found us in Rhinebeck, New York.
We ate at a diner, and it was the one dessert on the menu I had never had.

I loved the way the crust broke gently against my fork.
Had just the right amount of flour, sugar, and fruit.
When I closed my eyes, I saw bursts of blue while I chewed.
He laughed. It's true.

This no-bake recipe says all I need is mostly what I already have.
Sugar/salt/graham cracker crust/water.
Cornstarch and whipped cream.
Just cook half the berries, fold the ingredients together with a spoon, pour them gently into the crust.
Let it chill in the fridge.

I'm about to go to the store
for one more container of blueberries and the cornstarch
before this April snow falls,
even though I love the way it crunches
underneath my size 10 feet.

I'm going to surprise him with a slice on his plate when he gets home.
I'll skip the whipped cream--he hates it. I don't.
I can't wait to watch him break off a morsel to taste
lift his fork to his mouthwatering lips,
drop his head while he chews,
hear him say:
Woman. This is good.

Fantasy

If I were the brave woman
I conjure
when I gaze in the mirror,

I would sail the Atlantic.

If I encountered
a pod of dolphins,
I would dive in,
see how long
I could swim apace.

Until that
surge of courage,
I have my seashells,
and their
echoes of
oceanic roar.

The Real

She is no
coffee-gulping precisionist
zipping from zero to sixty
from speckless home to work,
to gourmet meals,
uncluttered rooms,
cherubic children
without an unfrayed nerve.

Our heroine snatches
kes now and then
to read,
sit in silence,
write,
steep her softness
in a bath,

let a light layer
of dust collect.

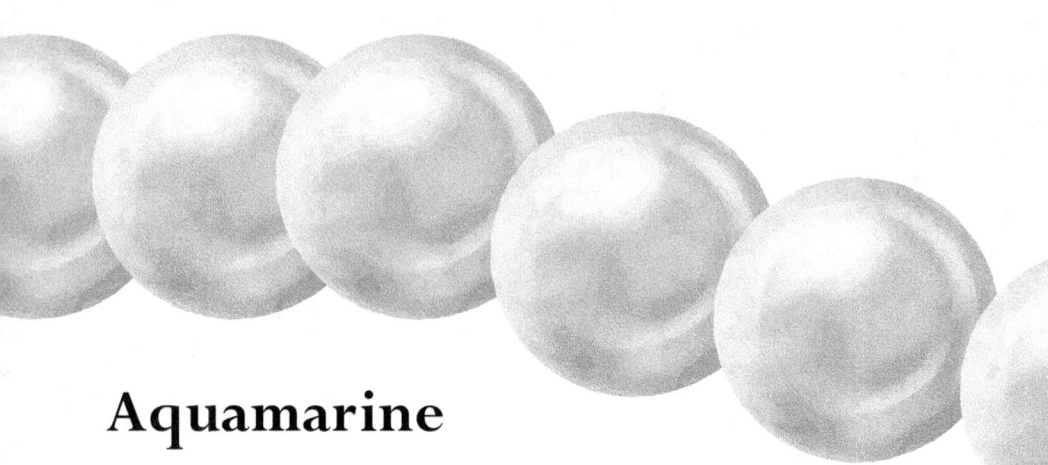

Aquamarine

One of these days
I will learn to swim.

Not just dog paddling
back floating
treading water

but super diving

arms tight against
my sides,
arms unfolding,
propelling myself
upwards,

butterfly stroking
like a mermaid,

my water trails
foamy,
straight,
sharp like scissors

emerging with
baby oil glisten,
hair, curves, bouncing,

breathing lightly.

Authentic Woman

Some men joke
we flesh and blood women
should fear the new
pouty-lipped robot women:
full breasts in perfect spheres,
always willing to be penetrated,
listening agreeably
to any and everything,
offering soothing words.

I am unafraid.
Nothing like
the circle of my arms,
my whispered "love yous"
to make his confidence bloom,
bluster.

Whet

Don't need
misty
crystal-ball
magic
when
we are submerged
in balmy water,
my back against your chest.

Candles exuding
vanilla,
jasmine,
illuminating
hushed darkness,

the drip of water
from the faucet,
the fuse of our
lips/tongues,
octaves,
in echo.

For My Valentine

Your love?
Like the moon.

Always whole,
even when only
slices of it may manifest,
like beautiful nights
of crescent moons.

The way you crack a smile
at my kiss,
the occasional flower,
massaging my aching back,
cups of tea for my colds,
checking the oil in my car.
Pay bills.
Hug my sorrows away.

When It's Love

He poured, jounced
gin,
juice of an orange, a grapefruit,
in the Boston Shaker.

Held her gaze through
his decantation.

She passed the quaff
underneath her nose:
hints of
juniper
cinnamon
ginger
coriander
and chocolate.

She put down the glass.
Straddled him.

"All I need is you
to feel a rainbow of fire."

Soothing Rain

My honey,
my heroine,
knows every sore spot.

The edges of her hands,
her fists
bang out the knots.

Her fingers
rotate in my shoulders,
my middle back,
lower back,
in looping motions.
Like cursive writing.

The next day
I am back,
lifting,
climbing,
lifting.

My honey,
my heroine,
who knows
every sore spot.

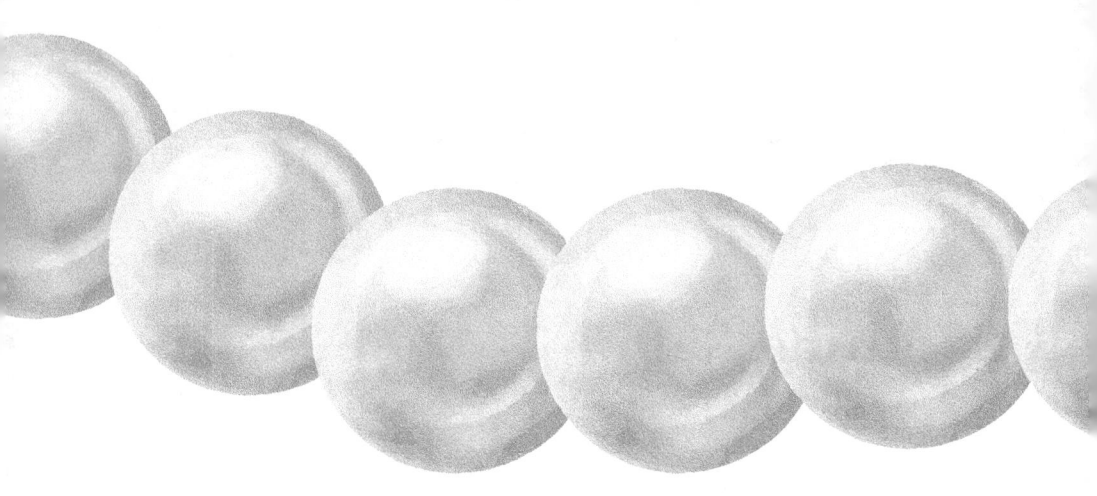

In These Middle Years

If somebody
slipped a thermometer
full of mercury between
our kissing skins,
where rivers of sweat
commingle,
its glass bulb
would burst open
like a steam pipe.

Our peppermint soap-downs
make me tingle
like his breath
in my ear,
and
I wistfully watch
proof of our passion
gurgle down the drain.

Dreaming of Summer

Every summer night
should be me
swinging on my porch
as the sun's upper limb
sinks in purplish haze
to the beat of a dragonfly's hum.

No scrolling through newsreels,
tapping pithy responses to texts.

Flute glass in hand,
peach wine almost to the brim
slow sips until starry skies
and moonrise.

Security

Snowy white garb is lucid
against brown skin,
but no more of it for me.

Too many garments ruined by
a splash of sauce,
brush of lipstick.

Bleach is insufficient.
Prissiness gorges too much time.

Why mask my penchant
for living fully,
eating vigorously,
sometimes laughing
or talking as I do?

A Sunday Morning

He drove us to
the ocean.
After we walked to the shoreline
he scattered petals of blue and red orchids
around my feet.

"We don't need an occasion
or ceremony for you to be so honored."

We locked fingers.
Watched my little garden
float away.

The current laved our legs,
seeped between our toes
and our feet sank deep in sand.

The aroma of salt
caressed our nostrils,
the backs of our throats.

A Summer Day in the Bronx

She wanted to breathe / swallow
sea air,
be cooled by the breeze.
I rolled my car windows
all the way down
as we meandered City Island Road,
and Orchard Beach.

Emancipated ourselves
from the clock, the GPS,
to roam Pelham Bay Park,
to tone with thickets of green.

When She's in Remission

There we will stand
our tresses coiled around themselves
like strands of DNA

two white roses
tucked behind each of our ears

Earth-brown lipstick
coloring our lips
mouths open
bucket-wide,
laughing.

We will dance.
Catch raindrops on our tongues
if it pours,
or saturate our pores in sunlight

Just because.

Trees of Everlasting Life

They are four stories tall now. Loved our pines
since I was six, and they were six feet tall;
especially the sprout of the young cones,
the cling of their stems and branchlets to their mothers' limbs.

I'd stroke their scales but
as much as I wanted them prickly in the fold of my hands,
I never liked taking from those
who don't want to give.

I waited until they
tired of opening and closing,
spilling seeds, receiving pollen,
and were released to the ground.

Fallen pine needles snapped in
withered surrender beneath our feet
as we collected pinecones
if they were dry,

open to us, to our pothering
over which was fullest throughout our Acquisition,
to receiving red/blue/green paint,
or glue, and gold or silver glitter.

If they were pretty enough, or
if your Mama loved you lots,
they were strung,
hung on Christmas trees,

like ornaments.
And with the coniferae outside our windows,
we struggled mightily with lights, tinsel, and wrapping paper
to mimic majesty.

Flip

I am a descendant of waste not, want not.
When my heart stops beating,
my cells gasp for air,
my veins evict my blood,

hope they'll put me in a biodegradable burial pod.

      As nitrogen/phosphorus/magnesium leak,
methane bloats my belly,
Death's sweet stink beckons blowflies
to eat and molt, eat and molt,
dissolve my flesh to sugar,

I pray I may feed a sturdy fir, a pine.

Whomever is left to cherish memories of me,
parse through my photographs and books--

Please.
Be more attentive than me.

Had a plastic bin on the floor of my closet,
holding a Ziploc bag inside with Nana's, Aunt Joan's jewelry.
While I was cleaning, I put it in front of my bed.
Tripped. Chunky gold earrings, bangles, bracelets, silver necklaces erupted.

My love picked them up.
Placed them carefully back inside.
You've got some nice pieces in here.

Costume jewelry mostly, I replied, with a wave of hand.
He held up a necklace.
        Rolled its beads around his fingers.
These pearls are real.

Nana passed in '86,
Aunt Joan in '95.

Had I known

I'd have long ago strung those pearls into a necklace
that would fall in a perfect drape
above the pulse of my throat

worn it with low-lying V-neck dresses,
off-the-shoulder blouses,
at weddings, parties
laughed often,
pressing my fingers dramatically by my bosom

wresting chance after chance
to give Daddy's mother and his sister
credit for this adornment,
brag about their homemade sweet tea,
good choices in men.

The Mother

With the flux of seasons,
morning suns gave rise to
low-lying fog and a hush that
fell over the lake like a shroud.

Along the shore,
a trumpeter swan
nudged her eggs
into the nest's center.

A man approached,
hoping to snap a photo
or snatch an egg.

He discovered her bill
was crystal-ball hard.

Once

He had a 45 magnum
in his nightstand.

Curious, she asked
if she could hold his gun.

It was neither cold,
nor easy to hold
like she thought.

She tried to imagine
pulling the trigger,
unleashing a river of blood,
a cold corpse nude on a slab.

She handed it back,
never held another.

One and a Half Million and Counting

Mustard, ketchup stains
are blotted away
with gentle dabs
of soap and water.

Crumbs are wiped up.

You can apologize for
white-hot words hurt feelings.

Heartbreak--
you can parse through what you fused together:
laughter, love, sorrows.
Learn lessons.
Love again.

But you can't aim, pull a trigger,
then resurrect the dead.

A Vegan's Dilemma

I've discovered--

each inhalation
of freshly cut grass
is the ingestion
of a verdurous cry for help.

Flowers wail
when their leaves are cut.

Vegetables
can hear themselves
being chewed.

I too,
am reaper,
of murderous trails
with every flick
of my knife,
use of a plate,
or vase
on my table.

Happiness's Whisper

Those who swaddled us
in blankets, love,
will die.

Those who promised
forever
may leave.

Skin cracks.

Hair surrenders
its teddy-bear softness.

Bare skin under sheets,
daily awakenings,
sun rays,
raindrops,
snowflakes,
bus driver's good mornings,

happiness,
beauty,
are like that
newborn smell.

March 8

Today was International Women's Day.

When I got home and undressed,
found a hole had burst through the left thigh of my jeans.
This pair lasted less than a year,
and others are already pilling up.
It's great to have our feminine achievements celebrated worldwide
but in this cold weather
what I could use are denims
with cotton fibers tough enough
to honor these thickset thighs
that make music
brushing against each other when I walk,
these gatekeepers that bulge and kiss,
that hug my man,
make him hum in half notes.

Maybe I have sinned,
thinking this Western garb was meant for a sister like me
who never had the
pert rounded breasts
flat bellied, cinched-in waist
hourglass hips
bottom shaped like an apple or onion
to fit in with the clan of the slim thick.

Time for another trip to Fulton Street in Brooklyn.
The fabric of Moshood's pants/tops/dresses
flow around me like a zephyr,
finesse my curves,
forgive my bulges,
free my thickset thighs
to kiss.

Hindsight

Stop slouching,
she'd scold.
Mother said I would end up
with bad posture.
She taught me
to have pride
but
had I known
how much/how long
I'd need to be on my feet
fighting to be full
as a
Black human being,
woman,
mother,
teacher,
free from fear
of badges,
brute force,
budget cuts,

I'd have spent every night
like the doctor said,
with rounded shoulders
pressed against the wall
neck straight as a lightning rod
and practiced
standing tall.

Good, For Nothing

Sometimes these platforms and apps
are good-for-nothing:

When 10-year-old Ashwanty Davis feels like the only thing
she can possibly do
is hang herself in her closet
after her fight gets posted Musical.ly,

When small-town Minnesota City Councilman and Sheriff Tom McBroom
tweets
Diamond Reynolds
will blow the $800,000 settlement for Philando
in six months on crack cocaine--
he sees them come to court over lost children
dressed to the nines with Michael Kors purses
and not a pot to piss in--

it's time to talk about
these words,
images
that misrepresent,
maim,
kill,

Do something.

Me, Too

A movement Tarana Burke began
because a 13-year-old black girl
saw kinship, compassion, in Tarana's twenty-something face,
hoping she would help her, somehow,
with her stepfather's sexual abuse,
not knowing Tarana hadn't faced her own trauma.
Baby, I can't help you.
And later, Tarana said to herself,
Why couldn't I just have said Me Too?

And I Too,
like many of my sisters,
was unsurprised Tarana
was omitted from the cover for
Time's Person of the Year.

After 400 years
invisibility can feel
like that dripping faucet
the landlord won't fix.
If you're not careful,
you learn to sleep
to the rhythm of
wet taps on porcelain.

Last season
I saw some
black girls were dyeing
their kinky coily hair silver,
worn in twist-outs,
their strands splayed from
the roots like starbursts.
I laughed at them,
wishing we could exchange--
my graying tresses
for their youthful,
formerly black ones--
and in my derision
I never considered
these girls were in rebellion,

that through their hair
they exclaimed:
See me!
Hear me!
I too, am wise,

that I Too,
like Tarana,
could listen to,
learn from,
my beautiful, black
little sisters.

For Bella

As I gaze at your photograph--
shiny light brown eyes/
wide smile,
I wonder if the same hands
that meticulously
strung beads in your cornrows
were the same
that soaped your skin,
saw bruises,
and said/did nothing.

Things

Lasted 45 seconds
before I shut the video off.
It was her scream
rattling my ears,
the sight of Denise Collins' right arm
in the police K-9's jaw.

Tried to watch it
a second time,
sound muted.
Clicked pause
after five seconds
of her mouth, her eyes
opened wide,
twisted in terror.
Took two tissues
to wipe away
my tears, their salt stuck to
the lenses of my glasses,
before I could finish writing this
about another black body,
an innocent one,
belonging to a 52-year-old woman
whose left hand was amputated
when she was a baby,
badly injured in a fire.

The dog's name is Gabe.
Short for Gabriel?
The name means "God's messenger".
He was the angel who
told Mary about the coming of Jesus.
Police had him on a 20-foot leash,
looking for two robbery suspects.

That September morning,
Ms. Collins had been

behind her own home in St. Paul
(what kind of letter might he have written about this).

Gabe's bite so strong,
he pulled her out of her shoes.

The police assisted her immediately,
but Gabe tightened his grip on her arm at first,
as if seized by spirits of his brother bloodhounds--
I finally got one,
and I'm not letting go,
there's no rabbit grease,
muddy water,
knives,
to stop me.

Police went to visit her in the hospital,
apologized, and
Police Chief Todd Axtell's heart,
was broken by the footage.
And who knows why
officers let the dog walk around
a blind corner in a residential area,
first in line.

Ms. Collins is suing
Officer Thaddeus Smith.
Couldn't even change
her dressings herself.
Nothing will make the bite marks
on her right arm,
lower left leg disappear,
and I
am adding
taking out one's own trash
to the lengthening list
of things I cannot safely do.

Appropriation of Despair

Sweat-drenched twelve-hour days.
Tattered clothes, or none.
Slow / weary: lick of whip.
Citrus, hot ash, salt peppers poured over sliced skin.
Hungry? "Steal" a little cane, be fitted with tin muzzle.

Prefer suicide to seeing half your fellow Africans die,
you would be a zombie,
doomed spirit wandering Hispaniola.
Banished from lan guinee,
rest,
peace.

Mea Culpa

The Crescent City.
As a collegiate tourist,
visited Marie Laveau's grave.

Guide announced:
To make a wish,
scratch three X's on her tomb,
spin three times.

Hadn't known
to offer
flowers
coins
beads
rum.

My invocation? Forgotten.

If I offended
The Queen,
may she grant me
a blank slate.

Discovery

A 10,000-year-old caveman
was found in South America last year.

Cicero Moraes studied its skull.
His rendering--
Apiuna--
has African features,
like Luzia, who was 11,500.

Before Abu Bakari II and his 2000 boats.
Before the Vikings.

Wasn't just the Middle Passage
leaving our African bones/blood
in the coasts/arteries of the Atlantic.

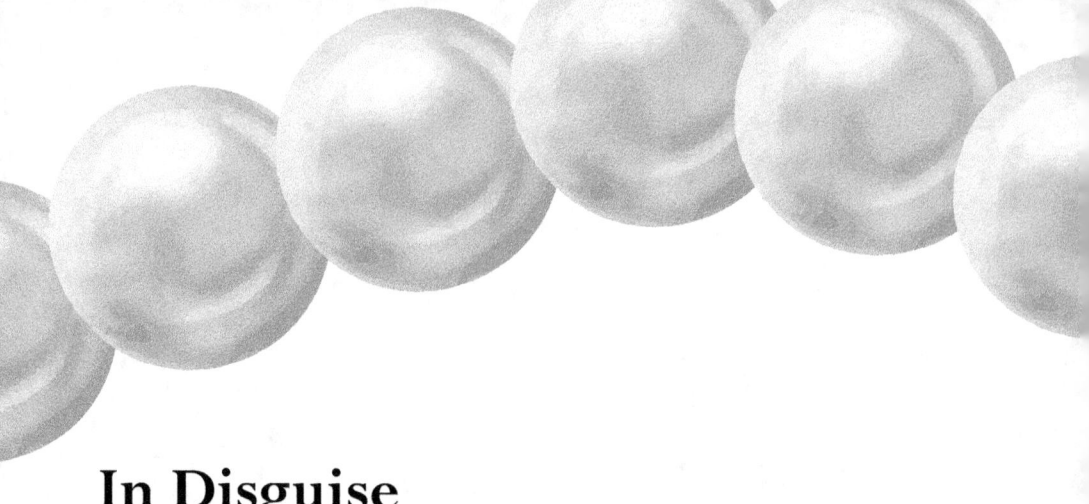

In Disguise

Two weeks to go
before our trip to see
I Am Not Your Negro,
they cried,
"Let us see the trailer!"

Baldwin appeared onscreen,
he hadn't yet uttered a word,
and one of my girls--
razor-sharp wit and intellect,
round-eyed, ebony-skinned--
proclaimed:

"Yo, that nigga is mad ugly! I am not going to see that shit!"

Echoing laughter and a chorus of agreement.
They forgot all about the five weeks
they cursed Mrs. Hunt for hating her darkest child,
hoped Mrs. Rivers could convince Victoria Rogers
that her rapist was still out there,
wondered if Tish and Joseph ever raised the money
to get Fonny out of jail,
if Fonny recovered from Frank's suicide,
or married Tish and held their baby.

I cried out: He was one of the greatest thinkers of the twentieth century!

"I don't care! I still am not going to see that shit!"

I wish I'd thought to say
that his stepfather declared him
the ugliest boy he'd ever seen
but he still read every book in the library
and went around the world
holding America accountable
from his triumphant lips and pen
and
I've had plenty of peaches
with a dent, a bruise here and there.
When I bit into them,
my tongue tickled just the same.

Time Out

Overheard some fool:
Dark-skinned women
shouldn't wear red lipstick.

Since quick fists are prerequisite
to objurgating strangers on the subway,
I did not interject.
My cheeks, ears
were ablaze with shame all day.

After work I bought
black construction paper
(why must drawing paper always be white)
and gel markers.

The box promised bright colors on dark paper.

Drew a rainbow
and a stick figure of me underneath,
a candy-apple red half-circle for a smile,
arms outstretched like a wandering albatross.

The reds, oranges, yellows, greens,
blues, purples, brown,
had me and that rainbow shimmering like Sirius,
feeling tree-bark strong,
caramel sweet

April 4, 2017

During class today, one of my students
asked about the Black Panthers—
I said that there are some different iterations of that organization,
but it's not what it once was.
And he said, Miss—
There will never be another Black Panthers.
There will never be another Dr. King.
There will never be another Malcolm X.

And I said, You're right. These are different times.
We will have different leaders.
Maybe you will be one of them.
Miss. This generation is messed up.

And just then
I heard a noise. Laughter.
Went to investigate
and forgot to tell him:
I see hope and promise and prosperity
in cedar skin and umber eyes.

Tomorrow, I will be sure to say to him:
Young soldier.
Let's not just mourn the bullet that struck Martin's jaw,
severed his spinal cord on this April day, 49 years ago.
As I am telling/teaching/showing you the works—
Toni Morrison and James Baldwin and Monique Morris—
Imbibe.
Arm yourself.
Run with it.

Homegoing

Cold plop of lucid ultrasound gel.
Doctor probed her protruding belly.
Said, "Everything looks good."
Perfunctory, "Do you want to know what you're having?"

"Not yet. We are going home."
Their beloved island, Jamaica.

They had decided that morning
they would not rear their brown baby
in the country that broke
Erica Garner's heart.

Case Closed: April 4, 2018

We got the crumbs
from the bread they devoured,
that we took from harvest to table.

When we wrested/were granted freedom
built homes/hearths
they licked their lips
passed restrictive laws
stole/burned property
lynched our men/women
to the roar of crowds
corpses hanging from oak/hickory limbs.

Assassinated our Prince of Peace,
and daily mock his dream.

Facade

They mean well
but sometimes I want to scream:
stop calling me strong.

If they knew
how much thread/
restitching
is required
to hold together
the top/wadding/back
of the patchwork quilt
that is my life,
how often I pop my collars
to camouflage
the throbbing pulse
at my throat,
how often I blink,
cowering tears.

Weight

That's not going to work, the woman said, pointing to Anike's outfit.
She was there to volunteer for our community garden.
Two other times that morning the ladies commented on her fitted jeans and halter top.
"But it's summer," I said, as Anike relayed this tale.

Just like the elderly women at the churches she's joined.
Pointing fingers, clucking tongues.

No inquiry about her interest in environmental justice,
gardening,
her internship at Wave Hill.

Had they talked to her
they might have heard about
the couch-clawing cat we all said she couldn't have
that she rescued from a shelter anyway,
the spinach she grows on the terrace,
the tomatoes and strawberries in her deceased mother's bedroom,
how she's prohibited my mother
from using paper towel and plastic shopping bags,
how botanical sexism is tied to suffering from allergies.

They always wonder where the young people are.
The way old people act, that's why.

"Do you want me to go with you next time?"
My fingers curled into fists.
No, Auntie, I got it. I know she does.

She is 22, 5 feet, size 2,
but like me,
she has full-blown fire in her throat.

"I felt guilty when Nana told me what happened.
We've argued about your clothing a few times over the years.
I only did that to protect you,"
recalling the gray-haired letch I scolded,
who stared her down and smiled when she was 12.

Then it occurred to me that the elderly ladies
from church, and the garden,
like me, were young once,
had men's eyes rove from head to toe,
sweet nothings turned sour on the street or worse.

Roses have thorns.
These women had upright posture and A-line skirts.

I'm only going to have this body for a little while.
Once I have kids I won't wear my clingy dresses and crop tops.

"Now who's body shaming," I said.
"Why can't mothers wear pum-pum shorts?"

Well one time I saw this mother with her little son and her shorts were REALLY short.
I don't think that's appropriate.

Isn't it funny how much weight we put on women.

Blue Funk

Warning:
this poem is ambitious.

The paper it was first written on
was crumpled in rage.

This poem is for
Saheed Vassell
age 34
father of a teenage son
who was killed
in broad daylight
on the corner of
Utica Avenue and
Montgomery Street
in Brooklyn
for holding a metal pipe
with a knob on its end
and pointing it at officers
in a two-handed
shooting stance.

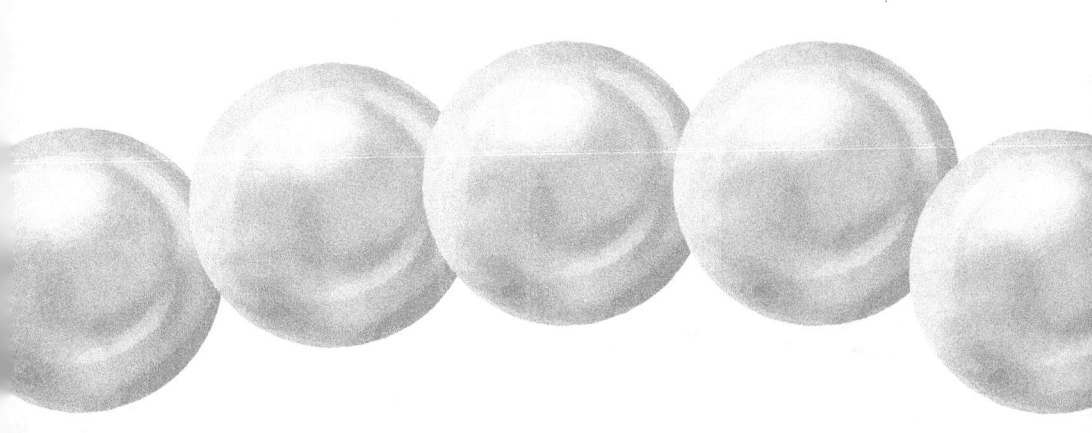

They thought it was a gun
and 27 seconds
after arriving on scene
without saying a word
they fired 10 shots.

Saheed was bipolar
refused to take his meds
had problems with alcohol
but was loved by
his family and community
for his gentle soul.

This poem is for
Keith Vidal, age 18, from
Brunswick County, North Carolina,
a good kid who was funny and
played ball and loved the beach.
He suffered from schizoaffective disorder
and though he took
anti-psychotics, he struggled.
When he called 911, his stepfather said
he was holding a screwdriver
and wanted to fight his mother.
Two officers calmed him down,
the third shot and killed him.

This poem is for
Deborah Danner, age 66
from Castle Hill in the Bronx,
an IT professional,
an active member
of Trinity Church Wall Street
who suffered from schizophrenia
and wrote an eloquent six-page essay about it.
A neighbor called 911
for her "erratic" behavior.
A paramedic talked the scissors
out of her hands, and then
Sergeant Barry arrived.
Didn't talk to calm her
and when she escaped
to her bedroom
she allegedly swung a bat
and he shot her to death.

This poem and its poet, cry,
knowing powerbrokers
are too greedy to care about
dismantling
the Eurocentric curricula
news coverage
media depictions
the prison-industrial complex
that dehumanize
people of color,
or fund
de-escalation training
crisis intervention
the hiring of more mental health practitioners
the building of more mental health care facilities
or
understand
anosognosia,
self-medication with alcohol and drugs,
and other reasons behind medication noncompliance.

Woke

Dipped drinking gourd into my well of memory.
Gathered poems from the eons, Phillis Wheatley to Margaret Walker.
For analysis. As mentor texts.
Found myself sitting alone in our virtual classes.

Gathered poems from the eons, Phillis Wheatley to Margaret Walker.
Found myself sitting alone in our virtual classes.
Why did I bother writing academically rigorous, culturally relevant curricula?
Then, day by day, the slow trickle of analysis, original poem-songs.

Why did I bother writing academically rigorous, culturally relevant curriculum?
"Would you like your poems included in an anthology?" I wrote.
Then, day by day, the slow trickle of analysis, original poem-songs.
"I'd love to get my poetry published", one student exclaimed through email.

Gathered poems from eons, Phillis Wheatley to Margaret Walker.
Found myself sitting alone in our virtual classes.
"Would you like your poems included in an anthology?" I wrote.
All this, from dipping drinking gourd into my well of memory.

Continuum

They think we can take it:

the strike of a baton,
bars of a jail,
the wars of our cells;
even hospitals do less to numb our pain.
That must be why Virginia state police charged
Robert T. McGee with one felony count of hit & run
and one misdemeanor count for assault
instead of attempted murder
for dragging Breeja Wilkins with his truck
after she had to pull over to check out a noise in the tire
and yelling back at him when he called her a nigger.
They had to graft skin
from the backs of Breeja Wilkins's thighs
to replace the skin ripped off her right arm and hands.

I have never seen anything so red.

VA State Police charged Breeja with a traffic summons
for being a pedestrian on the interstate
and improper stopping on the interstate.

Not much has changed since the 1960s
when my uncle was discharged
from the Army.
Fearing what could be--
his body battered/swinging
and my grandmother screaming--
he drove from Florida to New York
without stopping to sleep.
Slumped against the wall
when he got home.

A Daughter Speaks

Life for us in America
still ain't no crystal stair.

Those that wear the mark of the beast still thirst for our blood.
In lieu of cowhide, they whip out cell phones and dial 911
for swimming/sleeping/sitting/working out/barbecuing/
selling water/mowing lawns/inspecting real estate/delivering newspapers/
going home/ringing constituents' doorbells/
using a coupon.

They snatched Shane Holland's key fob
for sunning by his community pool;
at least he wasn't dragged to death from the back of a truck.
Did Schnatter's father/uncles/grandfather brag,
pull bloody bits of clothing floating in Mason jars off the mantelpiece, and
say: Look?
Now that he's resigned, will Papa John's remove him from the board, and his
Christian name for saying nigger?

Monkey juice.
In graffiti, in black, in white, on the storefront before Gourmonade's grand
opening.
Three days after, Vicktor Stevenson
was checking his security system.
A black man standing near a business in the Mission District
before 7:00 a.m.?
Four cops approached.
One with his hand dangerously near his hip.
Demanded he remove his arm from his coat.
Opened/locked the door as proof. Showed ID.
That night, his nine-month-old clung to him.
His wife awakened twice, screaming, crying, "No!"
He cradled her and their son. It's alright. I'm here.

DaShawn Horne wears a helmet to protect that part of his skull
that was removed to reduce the swelling in his brain

after Julian Tuimaga cracked his head with an aluminum bat
to teach his sister not to bring black men around.

American flag on his lapel, where his heart should be.
A handshake, a smile, strong and powerful denials
of American intelligence.
Voting bans for former convicts, strict photo ID requirements,
early voting cutbacks.
Towns seceding to maintain their whiteness.
Calls for race-blind admissions.
No transgender troops.
The Supreme Court upheld the Muslim ban
and struck down fair share union fees.
Fair Pay Order, overturned.
1.5 trillion-dollar tax cut for the rich,
seven hundred-billion-dollar military budget,
cuts to SNAP, WIC, and public schools with forty million in poverty.

Linda Daniels paid $1150 of her $1800 debt to PSE&G.
Please, her children begged before they turned off her power, then, oxygen tank.
She died gasping for air as her heart came to a stop.

Working poor shuttling from shelters to the streets on $8 an hour.
Even the middle class getting priced out of SoBro, SoHa, NoMa, and South Los Angeles.
Half a million in jail because they can't afford their bail.

Markeis Jr. and his siblings may cry because they saw
and his mother had no time to shield their eyes
while she tried to stop the blood from the bullet wound
but Michael Drejka will remain free.
The authorities saw Markeis Sr's shove,
were blind to his retreat;
he hadn't dropped to his knees.
Zimmerman still roams/raves/stalks;
the Justice Department reopened the Till case.

His killers are dead and Carolyn Bryant Donham,
with her forked tongue,
will not be joining the 2.2 million imprisoned.
Nor will Jeronimo Yanez,
Blane Salamoni,
Howie Lake II,
Walter Isaacs
or Joseph Weekley.

He clung to the doorframe as they handcuffed, tackled,
and forced him into the van:
I don't want to go to Honduras. It's better in jail. I'll die if I go!
As will "Joanna", who escaped here after gangs killed her brother.
ICE detained her husband.
She tells her American-born children: Your father is on vacation.
Brown babies cry in cages underneath foil blankets,
separated/adopted away from their mothers and fathers
so they might stop coming north of the border.

A Puerto Rican flag on her shirt.
A claim she had a permit for the space.
He was being asked to leave.
He swayed. Advanced.
Timothy Trybus pointed his finger at Mia Irizarry:
You're not going to change us. You know that?
You should not be wearing that! Are you a United States citizen? Are you educated?
"I'm feeling highly uncomfortable. Can you grab him, please? Officer?"
Officer Connor turned his back.
It could take another month before 11,000 in Puerto Rico have power.
When it gets too hot in their house in Yabucoa
Elogia Sepulveda drags her bed-ridden husband Jose
out to their front porch to cool off
and Flint still has 14,000 damaged lead and galvanized water service pipes.

Trying not to set down on the Courthouse steps
and throw up hands in despair
while these makebates do their work on our right
to choose when/how often to be mothers or
have health care.

But all the time, we keep a-climbin' on,
even though these times are mighty dark, and
shaming/shouting white supremacists out of restaurants
won't be enough.

But hope is a mustard seed.
It blows far and wide in the winds.
Sets itself down with mighty roots.

Memphis PD told that white woman caller that Michael Hayes could finish inspecting the house.
He's got a contract. He's in control. He can take all day.
If you interfere one more time, I'm going to arrest you.

Dr. Jennifer Schulte burst into tears
when the cops didn't stop the black folk from barbecuing.
The chicken and ribs were sizzling, the hot sauce was flowing,
and the bass was bumping at #BBQWhileBlack
as a great multitude did the Electric Slide to "Before I Let Go"
at Lake Merritt Park.
Jordan Rodgers went to Disneyland with donated tickets,
and Allison Ettel resigned as CEO of TreatWell Health.

Although Stephanie Sebby-Stempel was able to post her $65,000 bail and
was not shot for pushing and biting the officers
who came to arrest her,
she was fired from Rodan &Fields, and was charged with

one count of third-degree assault and battery
and two counts of assaulting, beating, or wounding a police officer
while resisting arrest.

Dr. Nnenna Aguocha was allowed into her home after her late shift and to get some sleep.

Timothy Trybus was arrested for assault and disorderly conduct.
Officer Patrick Connor resigned.

Officer Campbell called the complainant, and she apologized to Representative Janelle Bynum.

Camila Hudson's coupon was verified, and CVS fired Morry Matson.

The four black teens playing in Minnehaha Falls Park--
two 13-year-olds, one 14-year-old, 15-year-old--
that allegedly wielded sticks, knives, and a gun
were found to be unarmed,
are still alive,
the gravel/grit from sitting in the road in front of a police car
has been washed from their clothes, and
their mosquito bites have likely healed.

Facebook raised over $13 million for RAICES to reunite undocumented families.

Crowds are gathering,
voices like rolling thunder, eyes sparkling like glass,
demanding leaders whose words and deeds are trustworthy and true.

Alexandria Ocasio-Cortez unseated Joe Crowley,
London Breed is leading San Francisco,
Stacy Abrams is running for governor of Georgia.

I pray Uriah Sharp got the action figures he wanted
and one day resumes his paper route;
and DaShawn Horne will walk fluidly/speak fluently/
swing his son Deion in the air,
and his mother can stop crying.

I'm still going.
Even when I weep, I
try not to turn back or fall.
I take shelter behind the shield of His favor,
as the moneychangers and dove sellers yank at
the threads of what remains of this democracy.

May the day come when
everyone has a home and health,
making a false report will be a felony,
and
we black women can stop climbin'
flagpoles or the Statue of Liberty
for freedom's sake
or daring would-be assassins
to shoot straight, if at all.

-July 31, 2018

She Wanted To Become A Nurse

Like her mother said,
Breonna deserved so much more than
a law in her name
that bans no knock warrants,
requires commanding officer review and
approval for all search warrants,
affidavits in support of search warrants,
risk matrices before an officer can seek
judicial approval for a warrant,
a housing credit program
to entice officers to live in certain low-income areas in Louisville,
expanded random drug testing of officers,
and 12 million dollars for her family
after the lawyers take their cut.
Brett Hankison only got fired.
Officer Myles Cosgrove and Sgt. Jonathan Mattingly, on administrative leave.
Mayor Fischer cannot begin to imagine Tamika Palmer's pain.
America, the beau ideal of freedom and free enterprise,
Innovator of the three-fifths compromise
Fugitive Slave Act and slave patrols
The Black Codes and Jim Crow laws

Poll tax, literacy test, and Grandfather clause
Redlining and housing covenants
Gerrymandering
The Tuskegee Syphilis Experiment
Forced sterilizations
Shelby vs. Holder and gouging Section 4 of the Voting Rights Act
Remover of mailboxes
Great Defender against the fraud of early voting,
cannot begin to imagine us free.
As of September 20, 2020, Daniel Cameron has not charged the officers
who shot Breonna five times
with second-degree manslaughter.
Don't dare ask us
to retire the hashtags
put down our placards
or celebrate
the largest settlement for a black woman killed by police.

Closing the Gap

I was twenty the summer afternoon
I finally took Daddy's Last Poets album
from the front of its gold-plated album rack.

I turned the volume dial up until
Umar bin Hassan was hollering
niggers are scared of revolution and
Niggers fuck, niggers fuck, fuck, fuck
Niggers love the word fuck
think it's so fuckin' cute, they fuck you around.

My mother threw open my bedroom door,
eyebrows raised, her eyes wide opal orbs.

Turn that off!

I rolled my eyes
but the burn in her voice
and heft of her hands
made me shut off my stereo instead of asking
which word bothered her most
nigger or fuck
knowing it was likely both for this woman who wore
soft curls, white gloves, A-line skirts she sewed herself
when she was twenty.

Her opal orbs sparkled more than they ever flashed,
so I slipped the album into its sleeve,
back into the front of Daddy's gold-plated album rack.

Thirty years later, she did not remember that incident.
Today she listened to the song for the first time.
I asked her what she thought.
Her pause, a whole rest in 4/4 time.
A lot of what they say is true. They are scared.
What changed your mind?
Everything that's going on.
They should never have killed Malcolm.

Hold

Had been holding my belly in as I breathed.
Sought peace in a cup of sweet orange tea and honey,
a pen, and my journal the other night.
A red post-it note fluttered to the floor:
"I want you to write this down.
While I was under the anesthesia I dreamed that I was in the arms of Jesus.
God is real! Jesus is real!
I want to go to church.
I didn't realize how angry I was at God because I wanted Daddy to live longer.

***

We all had prayed before, during, after my sister's eleven-hour surgery
to cut out one quarter of her thigh and remove that tumor.
Two months of dialysis for kidney, liver failure.
Three months of physical therapy and her relearning how to walk.

***

They sent her home to me.
Daydreamed escorting Donna down the aisle at church to find a seat,
waving at our pastor, pointing at her and reciting Matthew 19:26.
Those three weeks, I juiced.
Fed her vegan meals and her pills.
Watched TV with her.
Laid next to her in bed to soothe her to sleep.
Pneumonia. Metastasis into her lungs, brain, and eyes.

***

Four hours of chemotherapy.
Neural toxicity. Temporary coma.
Donna woke up to the news that there was nothing else they could do.
All I could do was
watch the doctor tell my mother her youngest daughter
was going to die, and Donna tell her daughter.

Scanned her wrists for a pulse when her breath was faint and ran for the nurse.
Formed a ring of held hands with our family when her soul left her body.

***

As friends and colleagues filled the chapel,
bragged about how kind, smart, funny, loving, and skilled she was,
I wondered if God had chosen the wrong one.

***

Asked why Matthew 19:26 did not save
my 44-year-old sister from synovial cell sarcoma,
my nonsmoking 62-year-old father
who ate well and never drank from multiple myeloma.
My father's sister, from lymphatic cancer, at 49.
I turned 49 on June 18.
Will I be allowed to beat those odds?

***

There is Psalm 118:6, but I am
indeed afraid of these mere mortals
that may pull me or mine over,
break down my door,
shoot without survey,
video evidence, or no, saw me or mine open, look for drugs,
put our lives on display for dissection, judgement, justification.

***

From time to time I would think a heavenly reunion with Daddy and Donna would be better than living.

***

This virus hit.
I sheltered in.

Secured a supply of paper and cloth masks for my family and me.
No Clorox or Lysol left on the shelves,
I vacuumed, mopped,
wiped down countertops, doorknobs, light switches, and walls
until every room boasted vinegar and lavender.

***

Sipped turmeric or sweet orange tea with honey
mornings and nights as siren after siren wailed.
Avoided overexposure to footage
of bleary-eyed doctors and nurses,
body bags, and refrigerated trailers.

***

I swallowed the scent of cherry blossoms on my block,
walked amongst their fallen petals,
fell asleep to late night love songs by robins and hermit thrushes,
arose in orange afterglow,
gazed at the setting of the sun at my window.

***

Found myself
sucking icing from my niece's homemade chocolate cupcakes from my fingers
listening to my son's poems or raps
counting the books on my shelves I have not read
writing poems, promising myself not to stop
until my lines burn like hot grease in a damp frying pan,
hum like a dragonfly hovering over water.

***

I am cooking fresh food most days.
Reading every book I own.
A good girlfriend as long as he is a good boyfriend.
Returning to teaching this fall.
Daydreaming with my friends about restaurants and going to the gym.

***

My great-grandparents' eyes squint
against North Carolina sun and
pierce from their frame.

***

I will
remember the siren wail of black mothers and fathers
the tumble and crash of stone symbols of white supremacy
vote
sign petitions
e-mail or call politicians to keep
re-thinking and reforming laws and law enforcement.
Go back to the streets with placards in hand if it fails.

***

Used to search for Donna in shadows.
Not finding her saddened me but
that red post-it note did fall out of my journal,
a reminder to Hold His hand,
be comforted by His rod and staff,
keep walking these dark valleys
sip a cup of sweet orange tea with honey each night
inhale,
exhale
from,
and to the bottom,
of my diaphragm.

A Hymn To The Evening

After Phyllis Wheatley's Hymn to the Evening

7:00.

I love the stillness in the mornings,
caress of newly clean air,
but this daylong silence makes this Bronx girl miss
rap/reggae/bachata bass of passing cars
and the shudder of my bedroom window.

I stare at the steely sky,
wonder if my neighbors are tired of our daily salute.
Dwindling whistles,
fewer arms sticking out of windows
smacking spoons against pots.

I stroke the bottom of my metal mixing bowl
and the hundred tiny cuts etched in it
from three months of me and this old knife.

I like keeping things shiny and smooth
but these marks
in the bottom of my mixing bowl
remind me of grooves
grooves
groove
albums
Daddy's record player
pulling dust off the needle
to keep the records from skipping
Daddy head-bopping to
"The World Is a Ghetto",
stiff poppin' and lockin' to
"The Rubber Band Man" to make us laugh,
me asking myself where heaven was if it wasn't in the sky
and what made Ashford and Simpson
ooh, oh like that at the end of "Somebody Told A Lie"
Aretha wailing "Mary Don't You Weep"
while Daddy made pancakes.
7:01.

whistles
whoops
and the man several floors below
who cups his hands around his mouth
to make his woof woof bounce off our buildings.

I run to my kitchen window
push it all the way up
slip my arms
mixing bowl
knife
through my window guards,
get to banging,
clanging,
help my neighbors
make this music.

Seed

With red eyes,
red ties
splitting white shirts down the middle,
Proud Boys standing back,
and standing by,
no real stimulus in sight,

storm
Wall Street
in this modern-day Jericho.

Sow seeds of compassion.
Plant sycamores
from Pennsylvania Avenue
to Park Avenue
to Fifth.

Let the moneychangers,
the uber rich.
Scramble up the trunks.
Perch on the branches
beneath the throngs,

the homeless shuttled from hotel to hotel,
tenants that push furniture against holes in the walls and
leave food out to keep the rats at bay,
away from their babies,
workers that can't pay their rent,
residents who smell the mold in the walls
as soon as they walk in the lobby,

the students in schools without enough computers,
teachers who walked past the same dead cockroach in the hallway for a month now,
the hungry queued up for the boxes or plastic bags,
of chicken and vegetables so they can eat this week.

When the prophets come

command the moneychangers,
the uber rich 1%,

to make haste,
let the prophets abide in their houses,
give half their goods to the needy.
Let robber barons restore the masses fourfold,
pay on capital gains with glad and giving hearts.

And when the seeds of the sycamores
fall,
pick them up,

drop them in city street islands,
median strips,
and rat holes,
in front of office buildings, and
penthouses,
golf courses
mansion front yards and backyards.

Somebody plant a sycamore.

Afterword

These Pearls Are Real, the title of my fourth book of poetry, emanated from my poem "Flip", which I wrote to remind myself to cherish the legacy of life lessons and the heirlooms passed down to me by my family.

The poems in this collection also kept me sane.

The early years of the 45th presidential administration were frightening and extremely frustrating, as the politicians in his camp were determined to roll back the hard-won rights of women, people of color, and the LGBTQ community.

And then in 2018, my beloved younger sister Donna was diagnosed with synovial cell sarcoma at the age of 44 as well as liver and kidney failure. Watching her inexplicable suffering and her fight to live was heartbreaking and maddening, and I did not want to develop an eating disorder or otherwise hurt myself as I did when I lost my father.

When I had down time away from the almost daily visits with her in the hospital, consulting with doctors, and looking after my family, I wrote more love poems about family and romance. Writing exercises on Zathom.com's platform and my reactions to news stories about child abuse, sexual assault, racism, and police brutality became poems too.

When *These Pearls Are Real* was originally released in the Fall of 2018, Donna appeared to be on the road to recovery, and I was proud to share its publication with her. Although we lost her on November 20, 2018, this book is still testimony that creative energy is sustenance in times of sorrow.

Thank you for reading.

The Author

Carla M. Cherry is a native of the Bronx, NY. A graduate of Spelman College, New York University, and Lehman College, she has been teaching in the New York City public schools since 1996. Her poetry has appeared in various publications, including Anderbo, Eunoia Review, Dissident Voice, Random Sample Review, Firefly Magazine, Picaroon Poetry, Streetlight Press, MemoryHouse, Bop Dead City, Ariel Chart, Anti-Heroin Chic, The Racket, and Raising Mothers. All five of her books of poetry were published by ii-Publishing, which includes: *Gnat Feather and Butterfly Wings*, *Thirty Dollars and a Bowl of Soup*, *Honeysuckle Me*, *These Pearls Are Real*, and *Stardust and Skin*. She is an M.F.A. candidate in Creative Writing at the City College of New York.

CONNECT WITH ME:

Email: carla.cherrybxpoet@gmail.com
Website: www.carlacherrybxpoet1.com
Facebook: @poeticchic
Twitter: @carla_bronxpoet
Instagram: @carlabxpoet1

Publication Credits

"Homegoing" was awarded an honorable mention in the March 2018 Zathom.com writing contest.

The poem "Things" appeared in Issue 9.3 of the Same as well as their anthology, Raising Her Voice: An Anthology of Women Writers by the Same, Volume One, edited by Rachel Holbrook.

"April 4, 2017" was originally published in Issue 2 of Wallpaper Magazine.

"March 8" was originally published in Issue 1 of Brine (May 18, 2018).

"When the Student Teaches" and "Good, for Nothing" were originally published in Issue VI of Broken Tooth Press's magazine Hollow.

"Woke" appeared in Issue III of Porucpine Literary.

"She Wanted to Become a Nurse" originally appeared in 433.

"A Hymn to the Evening" originally appeared in Global Poemic.

www.ingramcontent.com/pod-product-compliance
Lightning Source LLC
Chambersburg PA
CBHW070859080526
44589CB00013B/1136